This Journal Belongs to

_____

First paperback edition March 2019

ISBN: 9781798499405

Book design by Lauren Cooper

www.transformedlovely.com

And we all, who with unveiled faces contemplate the Lord's glory, are being transformed into his image with ever-increasing glory, which comes from the Lord, who is the Spirit."
2 Corinthians 3:18

You were created in God's Image. Fearfully and wonderfully made. You are his workmanship. Created by him and for him to do his good work. As you spend more time studying God's Word, he will continue to transform your life into his lovely image and his glory will shine from you to those around you.

This journal is designed for you to be able to study God's Word on your own. The following pages give general instructions and examples on how to use this journal to its full potential. If you would like further instruction on studying God's Word and how to use this journal please visit www.transformedlovely.com/biblestudyjournal.

Suggested Resources to assist you in your study:
- A Study Bible/Or Bible: A study bible has built-in commentaries, cross-references, and background on each book of the bible.
- YouVersion App/The Bible App
- Biblehub.com or the Bible Hub app. This app is a great source for the original text, commentaries, and looking up the original meanings of the words used.
- Bible Dictionary
- Soniclight.com

1. **Select and read the Passage of Scripture**

2. **Context.** When we begin to study God's Word it is important to put everything into context. Before we try to interpret what the passage we are reading means, it is important to make observations about what is going on in the text. It can be easy to pull scripture out and use it to meet our needs, but that is not how it was intended.

Here is a good place to start:

a.) The author: Who wrote the book you are reading?

b.) The audience: Who was he writing to and why?

c.) Atmosphere: This refers to the mood, tone, or feeling the author uses when writing.

d.) The setting: Time frame of when the book was written, or when the narrative took place. Where the book was written from, where the audience was located, or where the narrative took place.

e.) Cultural and Historical Background: Gather a general idea of what life was like in that time and location. If there are cultural, or historical references in the passage you are reading, include them here as well.

f.) Major Themes: The themes of scripture can change from verse to verse, in general, what is the main idea of the passage.

g.)General Observations: What are things that stood out to you in the passage you read? What happened before the passage you read? What happens after? Are there any cause and effect relationships going on? If...Then.. statements? Promises from God? Repetitions? You are not searching for meaning now, but recording facts, connections, and observations you make.

3. **Select a key verse to study.**

Book	1 John	Author	John (Son of Zebedee)
Chapter	1	Audience	Believers in West. Asia
Verses	5-10	Atmosphere	Assurance/Urging

Where/When: Time Frame/Setting

Ephesus AD 70-110. Possible a circular letter to the churches.

Cultural/Historical Background

This John is the same author as the Gospel John and Revelation. He wrote clearly to believers. John would have been in Ephesus during his later years. Many false teachers were causing doubt and fear in the church. Fear of their salvation.

Major Theme of verses

If we are to have fellowship with Christ and he live in us we must walk in the light, confess our sins, and live out the truth.

What stood out to me? (General Observations)

These verses have many contrasts and comparisons:
Light vs. Darkness
Lie vs. Truth
Walking with Jesus vs. Walking in Darkness
to have sin vs. To be without sin

Cause/effect: If we claim to be without sin...then the truth is not in us.
If we confess our sins..then he is faithful to forgive us.

Key Verse To Study

vs. 9: If we confess our sins, he is faithful and just and will forgive us our sins.....

Open my eyes that I may see wonderful things in your law.

4. Ask Questions. What are the questions you had as you read through the passage? What are questions you could ask to guide your study? After you have asked these questions the next two steps will help you answer these questions. Come back and record your answers. Keep in mind that your answers should not be based on your experiences, feelings, other opinions, but on what scripture says. You should also make sure that your answer fits within the context of the scripture and the observations you made. If you still struggle to find answers to your questions, you can consult biblical commentaries.

5.Word Study. Select keywords that relate to your key verse and questions you may have asked to do a word study. The bible was originally written in Greek or Hebrew. When a keyword or phrase seems confusing, it can be helpful to find what words or phrases other translations use, or to look at the original language and its meaning. Record the word in its original form, how the word is used in other translations, and its meanings.

6. Related Scripture references. This is also known as cross-references. Use the keywords you selected for a word study to cross-reference them with other scriptures. Scripture should always be used to interpret scripture and scripture will always agree with scripture. In seeking answers to your questions, search for other scriptures that back up, or amplify the passage. After reading these related scriptures, examine how those scriptures add meaning to the main text.

How can I know I have fellowship with Jesus?

How can I have forgiveness from my sins?

What is unrighteousness? In my life?

What does it look like to walk in the light? Darkness?

Key words	Original language/meaning/other translations
Confess	homologeó- To speak the same; to agree; to voice the same conclusion
forgive	aphiémi- send away, let go, release,
unrighteousness	adikia- injustice, unrighteousness, hurt, opposite of justice

Related Scriptures to key words	How do these related scriptures shed light on this key word or passage?
Matthew 10:32	If we acknowledge or confess Jesus as Lord, then he will confess us before the Father. Just as we confess our sins and he is faithful to forgive our sins.
Matthew 6:14-15	If we forgive others, the father will forgive us. (Let go of what they have done to us.)
John 7:18	Unrighteousness is found in those that seek their own glory. One that is true-righteous seeks to only glorify God.

Fix these words of mine in your hearts and mind.
Deuteronomy 11:18

7. Meaning. What meaning did I find from these verses? Ask yourself what the word said to you, what was God teaching you, what conclusions can you draw from the text?

8. **Application.** How can I apply this to me personally?

> **a. Purpose of the Passage:** 2 Timothy 3:16 says, "All Scripture is God-breathed and is useful for teaching, rebuking, correcting and training in righteousness." What is the purpose of what you read? Was it to teach? Rebuke? Correct behavior? Train in Righteousness?
>
> **b. Where I've been:** Consider where you once were. This could be a previous belief, a past sin, or suffering you have gone through.
>
> **c. Where I am:** Did this scripture teach you something? Convict you of a current sin? Reveal how to correct a current behavior or attitude? Or train you in how you should live and train you in righteousness?
>
> **d. Where I want to be:** What are you going to do to get there? God's Word is living and active, sharper than a double-edged sword. What are the specific steps you can take to align your life to God's Word and will?

WHAT MEANING DID I FIND FROM THESE VERSES?

In order to be righteous, or right with God, I must walk in
the light and confess my sin. Not deny that I have no sin,
but agree there is sin in me. When I confess my sin, God is
faithful to forgive me of my sin, and let it go. He releases
me from the payment that is due because of my sin,
because we are cleansed by the blood of Jesus.

HOW CAN I APPLY THIS PERSONALLY?

Purpose of Passage:
☐ Teaching   ☐ Rebuking   ☐ Correcting   ✖ Training

WHERE I'VE BEEN

I once walked in darkness and lived a life of sin. I walked
far from the light of Christ and chose not to acknowledge
my sin.

WHERE I AM

I am so thankful that I walk in the light and that I can
confess my sins before God and he will forgive my sins. I
need to confess the sin of laziness and failing to follow
through on work God has called me to do.

WHERE I WANT TO BE

I want to always stay in the light where he has called me
to be. To be more devoted to daily time in God's Word,
prayer, and fellowship with other believers.

*"Do not merely listen to the word, and so
deceive yourselves. Do what it says" James 1:22*

9. Memory Work. Select and write a verse to commit to memory.

10. **Promise to claim.** Did God make a promise in the passage you read that you can claim? Is there a scripture you can pray back to God?

11. Prayer. Discuss with God what you have learned and what God revealed to you.

Thank you so much for devoting time from your day to study God's Word. I pray God draws you in and blesses you through your time in His Word.

I would love to connect with you through email or social media. You can find me on Instagram @laurentransformedlovely or visit my website www.transformedlovely.com.

KEY VERSE FOR MEMORY

PROMISE TO CLAIM:

PRAYER

Your word is a lamp unto my feet and a light unto my path Psalm 119:105

Book   Author
Chapter   Audience
Verses   Atmosphere

Time Frame/Setting

Cultural/Historical Background

Major Themes of verses

What stood out to me? (General Observations)

Key Verse To Study

Open my eyes that I may see wonderful things in your law.

Questions I have/Answers I found

Key words | Original language/meaning/other translations

Related Scriptures to key words | How do these related scriptures shed light on this key word or passage?

Fix these words of mine in your hearts and mind.
Deuteronomy 11:18

WHAT MEANING DID I FIND FROM THESE VERSES?

HOW CAN I APPLY THIS PERSONALLY?

Purpose of Passage:
☐ Teaching   ☐ Rebuking   ☐ Correcting   ☐Training

WHERE I'VE BEEN

WHERE I AM

WHERE I WANT TO BE

"Do not merely listen to the word, and so deceive yourselves. Do what it says" James 1:22

KEY VERSE FOR MEMORY

PROMISE TO CLAIM:

PRAYER

Your word is a lamp unto my feet and a light
unto my path Psalm 119:105

Book   Author
Chapter   Audience
Verses   Atmosphere

Time Frame/Setting

Cultural/Historical Background

Major Themes of verses

What stood out to me? (General Observations)

Key Verse To Study

Open my eyes that I may see wonderful things in your law.

Questions I have/Answers I found

Key words | Original language/meaning/other translations

Related Scriptures to key words | How do these related scriptures shed light on this key word or passage?

Fix these words of mine in your hearts and mind.
Deuteronomy 11:18

WHAT MEANING DID I FIND FROM THESE VERSES?

HOW CAN I APPLY THIS PERSONALLY?

Purpose of Passage:

☐ Teaching ☐ Rebuking ☐ Correcting ☐Training

WHERE I'VE BEEN

WHERE I AM

WHERE I WANT TO BE

"Do not merely listen to the word, and so deceive yourselves. Do what it says" James 1:22

KEY VERSE FOR MEMORY

PROMISE TO CLAIM:

PRAYER

Your word is a lamp unto my feet and alight unto my path Psalm 119:105

Book   Author
Chapter   Audience
Verses   Atmosphere

Time Frame/Setting

Cultural/Historical Background

Major Themes of verses

What stood out to me? (General Observations)

Key Verse To Study

Open my eyes that I may see wonderful things in your law.

Questions I have/Answers I found

Key words

Original language/meaning/other translations

Related Scriptures to key words

How do these related scriptures shed light on this key word or passage?

Fix these words of mine in your hearts and mind.
Deuteronomy 11:18

WHAT MEANING DID I FIND FROM THESE VERSES?

HOW CAN I APPLY THIS PERSONALLY?

Purpose of Passage:

☐ Teaching   ☐ Rebuking   ☐ Correcting   ☐ Training

WHERE I'VE BEEN

WHERE I AM

WHERE I WANT TO BE

"Do not merely listen to the word, and so deceive yourselves. Do what it says" James 1:22

KEY VERSE FOR MEMORY

PROMISE TO CLAIM:

PRAYER

Your word is a lamp unto my feet and alight unto my path Psalm 119:105

Book   Author
Chapter   Audience
Verses   Atmosphere

Time Frame/Setting

Cultural/Historical Background

Major Themes of verses

What stood out to me? (General Observations)

Key Verse To Study

Open my eyes that I may see wonderful things in your law.

Questions I have/Answers I found

Key words | Original language/meaning/other translations

Related Scriptures to key words | How do these related scriptures shed light on this key word or passage?

Fix these words of mine in your hearts and mind.
Deuteronomy 11:18

WHAT MEANING DID I FIND FROM THESE VERSES?

HOW CAN I APPLY THIS PERSONALLY?

Purpose of Passage:
☐ Teaching   ☐ Rebuking   ☐ Correcting   ☐Training

WHERE I'VE BEEN

WHERE I AM

WHERE I WANT TO BE

"Do not merely listen to the word, and so deceive yourselves. Do what it says" James 1:22

KEY VERSE FOR MEMORY

PROMISE TO CLAIM:

PRAYER

Your word is a lamp unto my feet and a light unto my path Psalm 119.105

Book   Author
Chapter   Audience
Verses   Atmosphere

Time Frame/Setting

Cultural/Historical Background

Major Themes of verses

What stood out to me? (General Observations)

Key Verse To Study

Open my eyes that I may see wonderful things in your
law.

Questions I have/Answers I found

Key words | Original language/meaning/other translations

Related Scriptures to key words | How do these related scriptures shed light on this key word or passage?

Fix these words of mine in your hearts and mind.
Deuteronomy 11:18

WHAT MEANING DID I FIND FROM THESE VERSES?

HOW CAN I APPLY THIS PERSONALLY?

Purpose of Passage:
☐ Teaching   ☐ Rebuking   ☐ Correcting   ☐ Training

WHERE I'VE BEEN

WHERE I AM

WHERE I WANT TO BE

"Do not merely listen to the word, and so deceive yourselves. Do what it says" James 1:22

KEY VERSE FOR MEMORY

PROMISE TO CLAIM:

PRAYER

Your word is a lamp unto my feet and a light unto my path Psalm 119:105

Book   Author
Chapter   Audience
Verses   Atmosphere

Time Frame/Setting

Cultural/Historical Background

Major Themes of verses

What stood out to me? (General Observations)

Key Verse To Study

Open my eyes that I may see wonderful things in your
law.

Questions I have/Answers I found

Key words | Original language/meaning/other translations

Related Scriptures to key words | How do these related scriptures shed light on this key word or passage?

Fix these words of mine in your hearts and minds.
Deuteronomy 11:18

WHAT MEANING DID I FIND FROM THESE VERSES?

HOW CAN I APPLY THIS PERSONALLY?

Purpose of Passage:

☐ Teaching   ☐ Rebuking   ☐ Correcting   ☐Training

WHERE I'VE BEEN

WHERE I AM

WHERE I WANT TO BE

"Do not merely listen to the word, and so deceive yourselves. Do what it says" James 1:22

KEY VERSE FOR MEMORY

PROMISE TO CLAIM:

PRAYER

Your word is a lamp unto my feet and a light unto my path Psalm 119:105

Book   Author
Chapter   Audience
Verses   Atmosphere

Time Frame/Setting

Cultural/Historical Background

Major Themes of verses

What stood out to me? (General Observations)

Key Verse To Study

Open my eyes that I may see wonderful things in your law.

Questions I have/Answers I found

Key words

Original language/meaning/other
translations

Related Scriptures to
key words

How do these related scriptures shed
light on this key word or passage?

Fix these words of mine in your hearts and mind.
Deuteronomy 11:18

WHAT MEANING DID I FIND FROM THESE VERSES?

HOW CAN I APPLY THIS PERSONALLY?

Purpose of Passage:
☐ Teaching   ☐ Rebuking   ☐ Correcting   ☐Training

WHERE I'VE BEEN

WHERE I AM

WHERE I WANT TO BE

"Do not merely listen to the word, and so deceive yourselves. Do what it says" James 1:22

KEY VERSE FOR MEMORY

PROMISE TO CLAIM:

PRAYER

Your word is a lamp unto my feet and a light unto my path Psalm 119:105

Book   Author
Chapter   Audience
Verses   Atmosphere

Time Frame/Setting

```
┌─────────────────────────────────────┐
│                                       │
│                                       │
└─────────────────────────────────────┘
```

Cultural/Historical Background

```
┌─────────────────────────────────────┐
│                                       │
│                                       │
│                                       │
│                                       │
│                                       │
└─────────────────────────────────────┘
```

Major Themes of verses

```
┌─────────────────────────────────────┐
│                                       │
│                                       │
└─────────────────────────────────────┘
```

What stood out to me? (General Observations)

```
┌─────────────────────────────────────┐
│                                       │
│                                       │
│                                       │
│                                       │
│                                       │
│                                       │
│                                       │
│                                       │
└─────────────────────────────────────┘
```

Key Verse To Study

```
┌─────────────────────────────────────┐
│                                       │
└─────────────────────────────────────┘
```

Open my eyes that I may see wonderful things in your law.

Questions I have/Answers I found

Key words | Original language/meaning/other translations

Related Scriptures to key words | How do these related scriptures shed light on this key word or passage?

Fix these words of mine in your hearts and mind.
Deuteronomy 11:18

WHAT MEANING DID I FIND FROM THESE VERSES?

HOW CAN I APPLY THIS PERSONALLY?

Purpose of Passage:

☐ Teaching   ☐ Rebuking   ☐ Correcting   ☐ Training

WHERE I'VE BEEN

WHERE I AM

WHERE I WANT TO BE

"Do not merely listen to the word, and so deceive yourselves. Do what it says" James 1:22

KEY VERSE FOR MEMORY

PROMISE TO CLAIM:

PRAYER

Your word is a lamp unto my feet and a light unto my path Psalm 119:105

Book   Author
Chapter   Audience
Verses   Atmosphere

Time Frame/Setting

Cultural/Historical Background

Major Themes of verses

What stood out to me? (General Observations)

Key Verse To Study

Open my eyes that I may see wonderful things in your law.

Questions I have/Answers I found

Key words | Original language/meaning/other translations

Related Scriptures to key words | How do these related scriptures shed light on this key word or passage?

Fix these words of mine in your hearts and minds.
Deuteronomy 11:18

WHAT MEANING DID I FIND FROM THESE VERSES?

HOW CAN I APPLY THIS PERSONALLY?

Purpose of Passage:

☐ Teaching   ☐ Rebuking   ☐ Correcting   ☐ Training

WHERE I'VE BEEN

WHERE I AM

WHERE I WANT TO BE

"Do not merely listen to the word, and so deceive yourselves. Do what it says" James 1:22

KEY VERSE FOR MEMORY

PROMISE TO CLAIM:

PRAYER

Your word is a lamp unto my feet and a light unto my path Psalm 119:105

Book   Author
Chapter   Audience
Verses   Atmosphere

Time Frame/Setting

Cultural/Historical Background

Major Themes of verses

What stood out to me? (General Observations)

Key Verse To Study

Open my eyes that I may see wonderful things in your law.

Questions I have/Answers I found

Key words | Original language/meaning/other translations

Related Scriptures to key words | How do these related scriptures shed light on this key word or passage?

Fix these words of mine in your hearts and mind.
Deuteronomy 11:18

WHAT MEANING DID I FIND FROM THESE VERSES?

HOW CAN I APPLY THIS PERSONALLY?

Purpose of Passage:

☐ Teaching   ☐ Rebuking   ☐ Correcting   ☐ Training

WHERE I'VE BEEN

WHERE I AM

WHERE I WANT TO BE

"Do not merely listen to the word, and so deceive yourselves. Do what it says" James 1:22

KEY VERSE FOR MEMORY

PROMISE TO CLAIM:

PRAYER

Your word is a lamp unto my feet and a light unto my path Psalm 119:105

Book   Author
Chapter   Audience
Verses   Atmosphere

Time Frame/Setting

Cultural/Historical Background

Major Themes of verses

What stood out to me? (General Observations)

Key Verse To Study

Open my eyes that I may see wonderful things in your law.

Questions I have/Answers I found

Key words

Original language/meaning/other translations

Related Scriptures to key words

How do these related scriptures shed light on this key word or passage?

Fix these words of mine in your hearts and mind.
Deuteronomy 11:18

WHAT MEANING DID I FIND FROM THESE VERSES?

HOW CAN I APPLY THIS PERSONALLY?

Purpose of Passage:

☐ Teaching   ☐ Rebuking   ☐ Correcting   ☐Training

WHERE I'VE BEEN

WHERE I AM

WHERE I WANT TO BE

"Do not merely listen to the word, and so deceive yourselves. Do what it says" James 1:22

KEY VERSE FOR MEMORY

PROMISE TO CLAIM:

PRAYER

Your word is a lamp unto my feet and a light unto my path Psalm 119:105

Book   Author

Chapter   Audience

Verses   Atmosphere

Time Frame/Setting

Cultural/Historical Background

Major Themes of verses

What stood out to me? (General Observations)

Key Verse To Study

Open my eyes that I may see wonderful things in your law.

Questions I have/Answers I found

Key words | Original language/meaning/other translations

Related Scriptures to key words | How do these related scriptures shed light on this key word or passage?

Fix these words of mine in your hearts and mind.
Deuteronomy 11:18

WHAT MEANING DID I FIND FROM THESE VERSES?

HOW CAN I APPLY THIS PERSONALLY?

Purpose of Passage:

☐ Teaching   ☐ Rebuking   ☐ Correcting   ☐ Training

WHERE I'VE BEEN

WHERE I AM

WHERE I WANT TO BE

"Do not merely listen to the word, and so deceive yourselves. Do what it says" James 1:22

KEY VERSE FOR MEMORY

PROMISE TO CLAIM:

PRAYER

Your word is a lamp unto my feet and a light unto my path Psalm 119:105

Book   Author

Chapter   Audience

Verses   Atmosphere

Time Frame/Setting

Cultural/Historical Background

Major Themes of verses

What stood out to me? (General Observations)

Key Verse To Study

Open my eyes that I may see wonderful things in your law.

Questions I have/Answers I found

Key words

Original language/meaning/other
translations

Related Scriptures to
key words

How do these related scriptures shed
light on this key word or passage?

Fix these words of mine in your hearts and mind.
Deuteronomy 11:18

WHAT MEANING DID I FIND FROM THESE VERSES?

HOW CAN I APPLY THIS PERSONALLY?

Purpose of Passage:

☐ Teaching   ☐ Rebuking   ☐ Correcting   ☐Training

WHERE I'VE BEEN

WHERE I AM

WHERE I WANT TO BE

"Do not merely listen to the word, and so deceive yourselves. Do what it says" James 1:22

KEY VERSE FOR MEMORY

PROMISE TO CLAIM:

PRAYER

Your word is a lamp unto my feet and a light unto my path Psalm 119:105

Book   Author

Chapter   Audience

Verses   Atmosphere

Time Frame/Setting

Cultural/Historical Background

Major Themes of verses

What stood out to me? (General Observations)

Key Verse To Study

Open my eyes that I may see wonderful things in your law.

Questions I have/Answers I found

Key words | Original language/meaning/other translations

Related Scriptures to key words | How do these related scriptures shed light on this key word or passage?

Fix these words of mine in your hearts and mind.
Deuteronomy 11:18

WHAT MEANING DID I FIND FROM THESE VERSES?

HOW CAN I APPLY THIS PERSONALLY?

Purpose of Passage:

☐ Teaching ☐ Rebuking ☐ Correcting ☐ Training

WHERE I'VE BEEN

WHERE I AM

WHERE I WANT TO BE

"Do not merely listen to the word, and so deceive yourselves. Do what it says" James 1:22

KEY VERSE FOR MEMORY

PROMISE TO CLAIM:

PRAYER

Your word is a lamp unto my feet and a light unto my path Psalm 119:105

Book   Author

Chapter   Audience

Verses   Atmosphere

Time Frame/Setting

Cultural/Historical Background

Major Themes of verses

What stood out to me? (General Observations)

Key Verse To Study

Open my eyes that I may see wonderful things in your law.

Questions I have/Answers I found

Key words | Original language/meaning/other translations

Related Scriptures to key words | How do these related scriptures shed light on this key word or passage?

*Fix these words of mine in your hearts and mind.
Deuteronomy 11:18*

WHAT MEANING DID I FIND FROM THESE VERSES?

HOW CAN I APPLY THIS PERSONALLY?

Purpose of Passage:

☐ Teaching   ☐ Rebuking   ☐ Correcting   ☐Training

WHERE I'VE BEEN

WHERE I AM

WHERE I WANT TO BE

"Do not merely listen to the word, and so deceive yourselves. Do what it says" James 1:22

KEY VERSE FOR MEMORY

PROMISE TO CLAIM:

PRAYER

Your word is a lamp unto my feet and a light unto my path Psalm 119:105

Book   Author
Chapter   Audience
Verses   Atmosphere

Time Frame/Setting

Cultural/Historical Background

Major Themes of verses

What stood out to me? (General Observations)

Key Verse To Study

Open my eyes that I may see wonderful things in your law.

Questions I have/Answers I found

Key words   Original language/meaning/other
                                        translations

Related Scriptures to   How do these related scriptures shed
    key words   light on this key word or passage?

Fix these words of mine in your hearts and mind.
Deuteronomy 11:18

WHAT MEANING DID I FIND FROM THESE VERSES?

HOW CAN I APPLY THIS PERSONALLY?

Purpose of Passage:

☐ Teaching   ☐ Rebuking   ☐ Correcting   ☐Training

WHERE I'VE BEEN

WHERE I AM

WHERE I WANT TO BE

"Do not merely listen to the word, and so deceive yourselves. Do what it says" James 1:22

KEY VERSE FOR MEMORY

PROMISE TO CLAIM:

PRAYER

Your word is a lamp unto my feet and a light unto my path Psalm 119:105

Book   Author
Chapter   Audience
Verses   Atmosphere

Time Frame/Setting

Cultural/Historical Background

Major Themes of verses

What stood out to me? (General Observations)

Key Verse To Study

Open my eyes that I may see wonderful things in your law.

Questions I have/Answers I found

Key words | Original language/meaning/other translations

Related Scriptures to key words | How do these related scriptures shed light on this key word or passage?

Fix these words of mine in your hearts and mind.
Deuteronomy 11:18

WHAT MEANING DID I FIND FROM THESE VERSES?

HOW CAN I APPLY THIS PERSONALLY?

Purpose of Passage:

☐ Teaching   ☐ Rebuking   ☐ Correcting   ☐ Training

WHERE I'VE BEEN

WHERE I AM

WHERE I WANT TO BE

"Do not merely listen to the word, and so deceive yourselves. Do what it says" James 1:22

KEY VERSE FOR MEMORY

PROMISE TO CLAIM:

PRAYER

Your word is a lamp unto my feet and a light unto my path Psalm 119:105

Book   Author
Chapter   Audience
Verses   Atmosphere

Time Frame/Setting

Cultural/Historical Background

Major Themes of verses

What stood out to me? (General Observations)

Key Verse To Study

Open my eyes that I may see wonderful things in your law.

Questions I have/Answers I found

Key words | Original language/meaning/other translations

Related Scriptures to key words | How do these related scriptures shed light on this key word or passage?

Fix these words of mine in your hearts and minds.
Deuteronomy 11:18

WHAT MEANING DID I FIND FROM THESE VERSES?

HOW CAN I APPLY THIS PERSONALLY?

Purpose of Passage:

☐ Teaching ☐ Rebuking ☐ Correcting ☐ Training

WHERE I'VE BEEN

WHERE I AM

WHERE I WANT TO BE

"Do not merely listen to the word, and so deceive yourselves. Do what it says" James 1:22

KEY VERSE FOR MEMORY

PROMISE TO CLAIM:

PRAYER

Your word is a lamp unto my feet and a light unto my path Psalm 119:105

Book   Author
Chapter   Audience
Verses   Atmosphere

Time Frame/Setting

Cultural/Historical Background

Major Themes of verses

What stood out to me? (General Observations)

Key Verse To Study

Open my eyes that I may see wonderful things in your law.

Questions I have/Answers I found

Key words | Original language/meaning/other translations

Related Scriptures to key words | How do these related scriptures shed light on this key word or passage?

Fix these words of mine in your hearts and mind.
Deuteronomy 11:18

WHAT MEANING DID I FIND FROM THESE VERSES?

HOW CAN I APPLY THIS PERSONALLY?

Purpose of Passage:

☐ Teaching   ☐ Rebuking   ☐ Correcting   ☐ Training

WHERE I'VE BEEN

WHERE I AM

WHERE I WANT TO BE

"Do not merely listen to the word, and so deceive yourselves. Do what it says" James 1:22

KEY VERSE FOR MEMORY

PROMISE TO CLAIM:

PRAYER

Your word is a lamp unto my feet and a light unto my path Psalm 119:105

Book
Chapter
Verses

Author
Audience
Atmosphere

Time Frame/Setting

Cultural/Historical Background

Major Themes of verses

What stood out to me? (General Observations)

Key Verse To Study

Open my eyes that I may see wonderful things in your law.

Questions I have/Answers I found

Key words | Original language/meaning/other translations

Related Scriptures to key words | How do these related scriptures shed light on this key word or passage?

Fix these words of mine in your hearts and mind.
Deuteronomy 11:18

WHAT MEANING DID I FIND FROM THESE VERSES?

HOW CAN I APPLY THIS PERSONALLY?

Purpose of Passage:

☐ Teaching   ☐ Rebuking   ☐ Correcting   ☐ Training

WHERE I'VE BEEN

WHERE I AM

WHERE I WANT TO BE

"Do not merely listen to the word, and so deceive yourselves. Do what it says" James 1:22

KEY VERSE FOR MEMORY

PROMISE TO CLAIM:

PRAYER

Your word is a lamp unto my feet and a light unto my path Psalm 119:105

Book   Author
Chapter   Audience
Verses   Atmosphere

Time Frame/Setting

Cultural/Historical Background

Major Themes of verses

What stood out to me? (General Observations)

Key Verse To Study

Open my eyes that I may see wonderful things in your law.

Questions I have/Answers I found

Key words | Original language/meaning/other translations

Related Scriptures to key words | How do these related scriptures shed light on this key word or passage?

Fix these words of mine in your hearts and minds.
Deuteronomy 11:18

WHAT MEANING DID I FIND FROM THESE VERSES?

HOW CAN I APPLY THIS PERSONALLY?

Purpose of Passage:

☐ Teaching   ☐ Rebuking   ☐ Correcting   ☐ Training

WHERE I'VE BEEN

WHERE I AM

WHERE I WANT TO BE

"Do not merely listen to the word, and so deceive yourselves. Do what it says" James 1:22

KEY VERSE FOR MEMORY

PROMISE TO CLAIM:

PRAYER

Your word is a lamp unto my feet and a light unto my path Psalm 119:105

Book   Author
Chapter   Audience
Verses   Atmosphere

Time Frame/Setting

Cultural/Historical Background

Major Themes of verses

What stood out to me? (General Observations)

Key Verse To Study

Open my eyes that I may see wonderful things in your law.

Questions I have/Answers I found

Key words | Original language/meaning/other translations

Related Scriptures to key words | How do these related scriptures shed light on this key word or passage?

Fix these words of mine in your hearts and mind.
Deuteronomy 11:18

WHAT MEANING DID I FIND FROM THESE VERSES?

HOW CAN I APPLY THIS PERSONALLY?

Purpose of Passage:

☐ Teaching ☐ Rebuking ☐ Correcting ☐ Training

WHERE I'VE BEEN

WHERE I AM

WHERE I WANT TO BE

"Do not merely listen to the word, and so deceive yourselves. Do what it says" James 1:22

KEY VERSE FOR MEMORY

PROMISE TO CLAIM:

PRAYER

Your word is a lamp unto my feet and a light unto my path Psalm 119:105

Book   Author

Chapter   Audience

Verses   Atmosphere

Time Frame/Setting

Cultural/Historical Background

Major Themes of verses

What stood out to me? (General Observations)

Key Verse To Study

Open my eyes that I may see wonderful things in your law.

Questions I have/Answers I found

Key words | Original language/meaning/other translations

Related Scriptures to key words | How do these related scriptures shed light on this key word or passage?

Fix these words of mine in your hearts and mind.
Deuteronomy 11:18

WHAT MEANING DID I FIND FROM THESE VERSES?

HOW CAN I APPLY THIS PERSONALLY?

Purpose of Passage:

☐ Teaching   ☐ Rebuking   ☐ Correcting   ☐ Training

WHERE I'VE BEEN

WHERE I AM

WHERE I WANT TO BE

"Do not merely listen to the word, and so deceive yourselves. Do what it says" James 1:22

KEY VERSE FOR MEMORY

PROMISE TO CLAIM:

PRAYER

Your word is a lamp unto my feet and a light unto my path Psalm 119:105

Book   Author
Chapter   Audience
Verses   Atmosphere

Time Frame/Setting

Cultural/Historical Background

Major Themes of verses

What stood out to me? (General Observations)

Key Verse To Study

Open my eyes that I may see wonderful things in your law.

Questions I have/Answers I found

| Key words | Original language/meaning/other translations |

| Related Scriptures to key words | How do these related scriptures shed light on this key word or passage? |

Fix these words of mine in your hearts and mind.
Deuteronomy 11:18

WHAT MEANING DID I FIND FROM THESE VERSES?

HOW CAN I APPLY THIS PERSONALLY?

Purpose of Passage:

☐ Teaching   ☐ Rebuking   ☐ Correcting   ☐Training

WHERE I'VE BEEN

WHERE I AM

WHERE I WANT TO BE

"Do not merely listen to the word, and so deceive yourselves. Do what it says" James 1:22

KEY VERSE FOR MEMORY

PROMISE TO CLAIM:

PRAYER

Your word is a lamp unto my feet and a light unto my path Psalm 119:105

Book   Author
Chapter   Audience
Verses   Atmosphere

Time Frame/Setting

Cultural/Historical Background

Major Themes of verses

What stood out to me? (General Observations)

Key Verse To Study

Open my eyes that I may see wonderful things in your law.

Questions I have/Answers I found

Key words   Original language/meaning/other
                                      translations

Related Scriptures to   How do these related scriptures shed
     key words   light on this key word or passage?

Fix these words of mine in your hearts and mind.
Deuteronomy 11:18

WHAT MEANING DID I FIND FROM THESE VERSES?

HOW CAN I APPLY THIS PERSONALLY?

Purpose of Passage:

☐ Teaching ☐ Rebuking ☐ Correcting ☐ Training

WHERE I'VE BEEN

WHERE I AM

WHERE I WANT TO BE

"Do not merely listen to the word, and so deceive yourselves. Do what it says" James 1:22

KEY VERSE FOR MEMORY

PROMISE TO CLAIM:

PRAYER

Your word is a lamp unto my feet and a light unto my path Psalm 119:105

Book   Author
Chapter   Audience
Verses   Atmosphere

Time Frame/Setting

Cultural/Historical Background

Major Themes of verses

What stood out to me? (General Observations)

Key Verse To Study

Open my eyes that I may see wonderful things in your law.

Questions I have/Answers I found

Key words

Original language/meaning/other translations

Related Scriptures to key words

How do these related scriptures shed light on this key word or passage?

Fix these words of mine in your hearts and mind.
Deuteronomy 11:18

WHAT MEANING DID I FIND FROM THESE VERSES?

HOW CAN I APPLY THIS PERSONALLY?

Purpose of Passage:

☐ Teaching   ☐ Rebuking   ☐ Correcting   ☐Training

WHERE I'VE BEEN

WHERE I AM

WHERE I WANT TO BE

"Do not merely listen to the word, and so deceive yourselves. Do what it says" James 1:22

KEY VERSE FOR MEMORY

PROMISE TO CLAIM:

PRAYER

Your word is a lamp unto my feet and a light unto my path Psalm 119:105

Book   Author
Chapter   Audience
Verses   Atmosphere

Time Frame/Setting

Cultural/Historical Background

Major Themes of verses

What stood out to me? (General Observations)

Key Verse To Study

Open my eyes that I may see wonderful things in your law.

Questions I have/Answers I found

Key words | Original language/meaning/other translations

Related Scriptures to key words | How do these related scriptures shed light on this key word or passage?

Fix these words of mine in your hearts and mind.
Deuteronomy 11:18

WHAT MEANING DID I FIND FROM THESE VERSES?

HOW CAN I APPLY THIS PERSONALLY?

Purpose of Passage:

☐ Teaching   ☐ Rebuking   ☐ Correcting   ☐Training

WHERE I'VE BEEN

WHERE I AM

WHERE I WANT TO BE

"Do not merely listen to the word, and so deceive yourselves. Do what it says" James 1:22

KEY VERSE FOR MEMORY

PROMISE TO CLAIM:

PRAYER

Your word is a lamp unto my feet and a light unto my path Psalm 119:105

Book   Author
Chapter   Audience
Verses   Atmosphere

Time Frame/Setting

Cultural/Historical Background

Major Themes of verses

What stood out to me? (General Observations)

Key Verse To Study

Open my eyes that I may see wonderful things in your law.

Questions I have/Answers I found

Key words

Original language/meaning/other translations

Related Scriptures to key words

How do these related scriptures shed light on this key word or passage?

Fix these words of mine in your hearts and mind.
Deuteronomy 11:18

WHAT MEANING DID I FIND FROM THESE VERSES?

HOW CAN I APPLY THIS PERSONALLY?

Purpose of Passage:
☐ Teaching ☐ Rebuking ☐ Correcting ☐ Training

WHERE I'VE BEEN

WHERE I AM

WHERE I WANT TO BE

"Do not merely listen to the word, and so deceive yourselves. Do what it says" James 1:22

KEY VERSE FOR MEMORY

PROMISE TO CLAIM:

PRAYER

Your word is a lamp unto my feet and a light unto my path Psalm 119:105

Lauren Cooper is the author of Transformed Lovely. She is a former fourth-grade science teacher and now a stay at home mom to two strong-willed boys and a sweet little girl. Her husband is a youth and music minister in their hometown at Ninevah Christian Church, of Lawrenceburg Ky. She comes alongside her help-meet in ministry and leads small group bible studies for middle and high school students as well as adult women. Her favorite things are her family and friends, God's word, reading books, chocolate, coffee, and connecting with other women to talk about God's transforming love.

51473813R00083

Made in the USA
Lexington, KY
03 September 2019